NEWSBREAKS
for **STANDARD** English Learners
2024

◆ CONTENTS ◆

スポニチ/AFLO

■ホームランを打ち、ベースを回る大谷翔平選手
大谷選手は TIME 誌で 2021 年から 3 年連続で日本人の好きなスポーツ選手で 1 位を獲得している。2023 年 12 月、ロサンゼルス・ドジャースと北米プロスポーツ市場最高額の総額 7 億ドルで契約した。

■ジェーン・バーキン氏
歌手や俳優として活躍したジェーン・バーキン氏は、2023 年 7 月 16 日に永眠した。

BONNOTTE JEAN-PIERRE/Gamma/AFLO

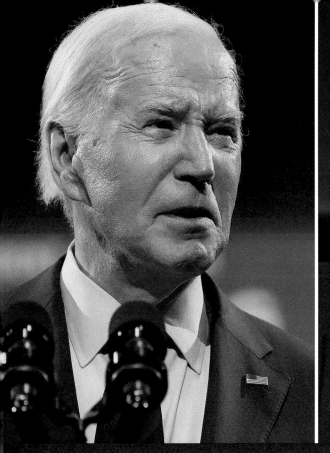

AP/AFLO

■ジョー・バイデン大統領（左）とドナルド・トランプ前大統領（右）
2024年11月に行われるアメリカ大統領選挙では、民主党はバイデン大統領、共和党はトランプ前大統領がそれぞれ候補者に指名されることが固まった。

■ノートルダム大聖堂の火災（2019年4月16日撮影）
2021年秋からスタートした再建工事は現在も続いている。2024年末に一般公開再開が予定されている。

REUTERS/AFLO

The Business of Sports

Shohei Ohtani could help baseball become more popular in the U.S.

AP/AFLO

Few people would doubt that Ohtani is the best baseball player on the planet right now. In 2024, he moved from the Los Angeles Angels, where he had been for six years, to the Los Angeles Dodgers. The surprising thing is that Ohtani will receive $700 million over the next ten years. This is the highest amount ever paid to an athlete, including soccer and American football players.

Sports is a global entertainment industry with huge markets, especially in Europe and the United States. It was mostly the United Kingdom that spread sports worldwide during the 19th century. That was because it had strong political and economic influence over many parts of the world. For example, soccer, which originated in the UK, is now the most popular sport in the world. There are professional leagues in more than 80 countries, not only in Europe but also in South America, Asia, and Africa. On the other hand, the industries of major sports in the United States have developed

---

NOTES

03. the Los Angeles Angels ロサンゼルス・エンゼルス	20. professional league プロリーグ	38. revenue [révən(j)ùː] 収入、収益
05. the Los Angeles Dodgers ロサンゼルス・ドジャース	25. independently [ìndipéndəntli] 独自に	43. as with ～ ～と同様に
18. originate [ərídʒənèit] 発祥する	31. Premier League プレミアリーグ	50. regain [rigéin] 取り戻す
	37. broadcasting right 放映権	59. the New York Yankees ニューヨーク・ヤンキース

■ クリスティアーノ・ロナウド選手

スポーツ選手の Instagram フォロワー数 1 位はロナウド選手で約 6.3 億人、2 位のメッシ選手は約 5 億人。大谷選手は 800 万人で野球界 1 位。ただし、フォロワー数には一定の bot（多数の偽アカウントを使ってフォローするコンピュータープログラム）が含まれていると言われており、人気を計る正確な数字ではない。

AP/AFLO

independently. American football, baseball, and basketball originated in the U.S. They are much more popular in the U.S. than any sport of British origin. The revenue of the professional leagues for each of these sports is more than 1.5 times that of the UK's Premier League, the world's largest professional soccer league.

With the development of media and the internet, the size of sports markets continues to expand. Each team earns a lot of money from around the world by selling the broadcasting rights to their matches. In addition, advertising revenue from companies is also a very large source of income. In fact, after Ohtani joined the team, the Dodgers started receiving advertising fees from many Japanese companies.

As with any other industry, there is competition among different sports. Baseball, whose professional league was established earlier than other major sports, was once the national sport of the United States. But now it has been replaced by American football. Major League Baseball (MLB) wants to regain baseball's popularity in the United States and develop its global market. Therefore, it has changed some rules to make baseball games faster and more thrilling. But what is needed most is a superstar on a strong team that will attract more attention. Ohtani has joined the top MLB team. The Los Angeles Dodgers has won the most league championships and has the highest attendance, along with the New York Yankees. Perhaps it is the MLB executives who are most welcoming to Ohtani in a Dodgers uniform. ■

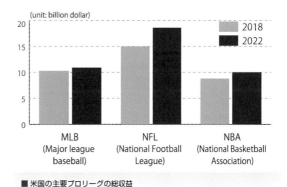

■ 米国の主要プロリーグの総収益

近年、MLB の総収益は NBA に並ばれており、NFL との差は拡大している。一方で、減少傾向にあった観客動員数と若年層の TV 視聴数は 2024 年から増加している。

■ ジョー・バイデン米国現大統領（左）と対立候補の共和党ドナルド・トランプ氏（右）

2024年3月、11月の米大統領選を戦う候補者を選ぶ予備選で、民主党のバイデン大統領と共和党のトランプ前大統領が党指名獲得に必要な代議員の過半数を確保し、両党の候補者指名が確定した。これにより2020年の大統領選で戦った2人が再び対決することとなった。

いずれも AP/AFLO

The 2024 U.S. Presidential Election
Who will Americans choose in November?

  In November 2024, citizens of the United States will choose their President. The Presidential election is held every four years. There are two major parties, the Democratic
05 Party and the Republican Party. Joe Biden, who is currently the President, will be the Democratic candidate. The Republican candidate will be former President Donald Trump.
10 The winner of the U.S. election is not simply the candidate who gets the most votes. There is a complicated system called the Electoral College that has been used for over 200 years. The President is chosen not directly by the citizens, but by people 15 called electors. The candidate who wins the most votes in a state gets the votes of all of the electors for that state. Because of this system, sometimes the results of the election are a little strange. In 2016, Democratic 20 candidate Hillary Clinton won the popular vote by almost three million votes, or 2.1%

NOTES

00. presidential election 大統領選挙	05. the Republican Party 共和党	16. elector [iléktər] 選挙人
04. party [pάːrti] 政党	07. candidate [kǽndədèit] 候補者	21. popular vote 一般投票
04. the Democratic Party 民主党	13. the Electoral College 選挙人団	57. hacker [hǽkər] ハッカー

of the total. However, Donald Trump won more electors than Clinton in states with large populations, such as Wisconsin, Michigan, and Pennsylvania. That is why Trump became President.

Many times in history, the Electoral College has produced much different results than the popular vote. Let's look at the 2000 Presidential Election as an example. In 2000, Florida had a population of about 16 million people, and it had 25 electors. Bush received 2,912,790 votes in Florida. That was only 537 more votes than Gore. However, he won all 25 of Florida's electors because he won the election there. On the other hand, New Jersey had a population of about 8.4 million, and it had 15 electors. Gore received 1,788,850 votes in New Jersey, and beat Bush by more than 500,000 votes. However, Gore won only 15 electors in New Jersey. This means that in these two states, Bush lost to Gore by half a million votes, but Bush got 10 more electors' votes than Gore.

This presidential election system is influenced by American history. Average people in the 1700s and 1800s did not know much about politics. The electors

州	獲得票数		選挙人数	
	Bush	Gore	Bush	Gore
California	4,567,429	5,861,203		54
New York	2,403,374	4,107,697		33
Texas	3,799,639	2,433,746	32	
Florida	2,912,790	2,912,253	25	
Pennsylvania	2,281,127	2,485,967		23
Illinois	2,019,421	2,589,026		22
Ohio	2,351,209	2,186,190	21	
South Dakota	190,700	118,804	3	
Vermont	119,775	149,022		3
Wyoming	147,947	60,481	3	
合計	50,456,002	50,999,897	271	266

■ 2000 年のアメリカ大統領選挙の獲得票数と選挙人数（選挙人数順）

were thought to be necessary to make better choices about who should be president. Today, the average citizen has a better education and access to more information. However, some of the information shared on social media is false. In the 2016 election, hackers in Russia and other areas created many fake stories about Hillary Clinton to support Donald Trump. In the 2020 election, a photo appearing to show Trump votes being thrown on the street spread on social media. However, the photo was from a completely different news article. Security experts believe that the same kinds of things may occur this year. And American citizens are still sharply divided on politics, religion, race, and other issues. Just like the past elections, the 2024 election is expected to be very close. ■

■ 能登半島地震で倒壊した鉄筋コンクリートのビル
能登半島地震では木造家屋だけでなく鉄筋コンクリートのビルが傾いたり、
倒壊するケースも多く見られた。

REUTERS /AFLO

Preparing for Disaster

It is difficult to make all buildings earthquake-proof

You may not realize it, but earthquakes are occurring somewhere every day. According to the United States Geological Survey (USGS), earthquakes that can be felt by people occur about 500,000 times a year around the world. Most of these earthquakes are of magnitude 3 or lower, which do not cause much damage to people or buildings. On the other hand, earthquakes of magnitude 6 or higher often cause great damage. According to Japan's Ministry of Land, Infrastructure, Transport and Tourism, 165 large earthquakes of magnitude 6 or higher occurred in Japan between 2012 and 2021.

NOTES

00. earthquake-proof 耐震性のある
03. the United States Geological Survey (USGS) アメリカ地質調査所
07. magnitude [mǽgnət(j)ùːd] マグニチュード
11. Ministry of Land, Infrastructure, Transport and Tourism 国土交通省
21. Great Kanto Earthquake 関東大震災
23. collapse [kəlǽps] 崩れる、倒壊する
27. Miyagi earthquake 宮城県沖地震
32. intensity [inténsəti] 強烈さ、震度
34. Noto Peninsula 能登半島
37. Suzu City 珠洲市

■ 関東大震災で全壊した民家

関東大震災の死者・行方不明者は約10万5千人で、火災による死者は約9万2千人。それ以外の約1万3千人のうち、住宅の倒壊による死者は約1万1千人とされている。

毎日新聞社 /AFLO

That is around 12% of the total earthquakes in the world. This means Japan is one of the countries with the greatest number of large earthquakes.

The Japanese government sets earthquake resistance standards that buildings must meet. After the 1923 Great Kanto Earthquake, in which more than 100,000 buildings collapsed, these standards became stricter. Since 1950, earthquake resistance standards have been changed about once every ten years. Then, three years after the 1978 Miyagi earthquake, in which more than 7,000 buildings were completely or partially destroyed, the standards were raised significantly. The new standards were meant to protect buildings from collapse even in an earthquake of about intensity 7.

On January 1, 2024, a major intensity 7 earthquake occurred on the Noto Peninsula. About 30,000 buildings were completely or partially destroyed in that earthquake, and about 260 people died. In Suzu City, about 40% of the houses collapsed. Most of these houses were built according to earthquake resistance standards before 1981. However, some buildings that met the new standards also collapsed. This is probably because dozens of earthquakes occurred in those areas in the two years from 2021. Naturally, the more earthquakes there are, the more damage buildings will suffer.

While newly built structures must meet the latest earthquake resistance standards, there are many buildings, especially in rural areas, that do not. In urban areas, people move around a lot and land prices are high, so buildings are frequently rebuilt. However, in areas where the population is declining and aging, buildings are rebuilt less often. Many local governments have systems to cover part of the cost of earthquake-resistant construction for buildings. However, these are not widely used because this construction takes time and requires lots of money. Although Japan needs to increase the number of earthquake-proof buildings, this will be extremely difficult to achieve. ■

WANT TO LEARN MORE?

Website　アメリカ地質調査所（英語）- https://www.usgs.gov/
Book　　井出 哲著『絵でわかる地震の科学』講談社
Book　　日経ホームビルダー編『なぜ新耐震住宅は倒れたか 変わる家づくりの常識』日経 BP

VOICE DL

Balancing Freedom and Security

TikTok has one billion users – but is it dangerous?

■ TikTok

TikTok は 15 〜 60 秒の動画を撮影し、それを簡単に編集・投稿できるアプリで、投稿されている動画は歌やダンス、子供の成長記録、趣味に関するものなど多岐にわたる。

REUTERS/AFLO

Many social media apps have appeared in the last 20 years. Among these, TikTok is a relatively newer app. It was launched in 2017, but it has very quickly become one of the world's most popular apps. As of 2023, it has 1 billion monthly active users, which is about 20% of the world's internet users. What is more, most of its users are young. ₀₅

NOTES

01. app [ǽp] アプリ（application の略語）	11. algorithm [ǽlgərìðəm] アルゴリズム （計算・問題解決の手順）	47. regardless of 〜 〜に関係なく
03. relatively [rélətivli] 比較的（に）	22. go viral （インターネットや口コミで	48. accurate [ǽkjurət] 正確な
05. as of 〜 〜現在で、〜の時点で	情報が）急速に広まる	50. altogether [ɔ̀ːltəgéðər] 完全に、すっかり
06. active user アクティブユーザー（定 期的に利用している人）	26. amateur [ǽmətʃùər] アマチュアの	
	43. spread [spréd] 拡散	

■ **imase**

imase は TikTok の投稿がきっかけでデビューしたアーティストの 1 人である。2021 年 5 月に「音楽経験 0 の素人がオリジナル曲を作ってみた」という投稿をし、その 7 か月後にはメジャーデビューを果たした。デビュー曲は現在 5 億回以上再生されている。

Kodansha/AFLO

According to a 2022 study, 67% of U.S. teenagers aged 13 to 17 use the app.

TikTok is unique because of its algorithm. As you watch videos on TikTok, it learns the things you like to see. Then it automatically recommends other videos that may interest you. "The TikTok algorithm knows me better than I know myself," said one user. As videos become more popular, they get recommended to more and more users. In this way, TikTok can spread a video very widely, and very quickly. This can lead to larger effects in popular culture, such as songs becoming big hits after going viral on TikTok. It can also be used to spread information about products or political ideas. For these reasons, all kinds of people, from amateur musicians to government officials, are very interested in using it.

Because it is so widely used, there are concerns about TikTok's safety. One concern is about the security of personal data. Apps on our phones can access our location, photos, and other personal information. TikTok is owned by a Chinese company, and the Chinese government can ask any Chinese company to give it access to user information. TikTok says that it does not share information with the government. However, people are worried that TikTok may not be able to keep this promise. As a result, many countries have banned the use of TikTok on government workers' phones.

Another concern about TikTok is the spread of false or harmful information. This is a concern with all social media, especially X (Twitter), Facebook, and Instagram. However, TikTok's algorithm makes it easy for videos to spread, regardless of whether or not their content is safe or accurate. Because so many children use TikTok, some adults want to ban the app altogether. On the other hand, a TikTok ban could limit people's freedom of speech. Finding the balance between security and freedom is an important issue in the internet age. ■

WANT TO LEARN MORE?

Website   TikTok - https://www.tiktok.com/
Book   日経エンタテインメント！編『TikTok ショート動画革命』日経 BP
Book   黄 未来著『TikTok 最強の SNS は中国から生まれる』ダイヤモンド社

VOICE DL

Rising Again

The Notre Dame Cathedral is being rebuilt

■ 骨組みが完成した修復中のノートルダム大聖堂（2024年1月15日）
修復作業を行う作業員が笑顔で手を振るこの写真は、X（旧Twitter）でシェアされ、多くの祝福の声が寄せられた。屋根の先端には祝いの花束が飾られている。

REUTERS/AFLO

When the Notre Dame Cathedral burned down in April 2019, it was a huge shock. The cathedral was loved all over the world as the symbol of Paris. It also got about 12 million visitors a year. No other historical place in Europe received that many visitors. "We cannot imagine a Paris without Notre Dame," said the French Heritage Society.

Right away, France's president Emmanuel Macron promised that the cathedral would

05

10

NOTES

00. cathedral [kəθíːdrəl] 大聖堂
00. rebuild [rìːbíld] 再建する
08. heritage [hérətidʒ] 遺産
09. Emmanuel Macron
　　エマニュエル・マクロン
16. lead [léd] 鉛

22. lockdown [lákdàun]
　　ロックダウン、封鎖
25. donation [dounéiʃən] 寄付（金）
26. spire [spáiər] 尖塔（せんとう）
32. the French Revolution
　　フランス革命

33. Victor Hugo　ヴィクトル・ユーゴー
33. *The Hunchback of Notre Dame*
　　(*Notre-Dame de Paris*)『ノートルダ
　　ムのせむし男（ノートルダム・ド・パリ）』
38. reconstruction [rìːkənstrʌ́kʃən]
　　再建

■ 炎をあげて燃えるノートルダム大聖堂（2019年4月15日）
火は出火から9時間後に消し止められた。ノートルダム大聖堂の象徴であった尖塔が焼け落ち、屋根の3分の2が消失したが、イエス・キリストが十字架に磔（はりつけ）にされた際にかぶっていたとされる「いばらの冠」などの所蔵品は、火災直後に消防士に運び出されて無事だった。火災の原因は現在も特定できていない。

USA TODAY Network/AFLO

be rebuilt within five years. Some people thought that the goal was impossible. Workers had difficulty rebuilding the cathedral for various reasons. The roof had been almost completely destroyed. Large amounts of lead were also used in the roof, and this lead melted in the fire. Lead is very dangerous for people, so workers had to wait for some time. High winds in the first winter after the disaster made the work dangerous. The next year, France was on lockdown during the COVID-19 pandemic. After it became safe to work, about 500 people worked on the cathedral every day. With hard work and donations from all over the world, the cathedral's famous spire rose again in December 2023.

The work on the original Notre Dame Cathedral was started in 1163. It took more than 100 years to finish. Over time, the cathedral was damaged by nature and by people in the French Revolution. In 1831, the writer Victor Hugo wrote a novel called *The Hunchback of Notre Dame* (*Notre-Dame de Paris*). This story about the bell ringer of the cathedral became very popular. People cared about the cathedral again and wanted to repair it. A reconstruction project lasted until 1864 and made the cathedral very popular again.

Notre Dame is scheduled to reopen in December 2024. Visitors to France for the Paris 2024 Summer Olympics will not be able to enter the cathedral. However, they will be able to see its spire from far away. Work on the outside of the cathedral will continue for a few more years. After it is finished, Notre Dame will live on as the symbol of Paris. ■

■ 新しい尖塔に取り付けられた風見鶏（2023年12月16日）
以前設置されていた風見鶏は大きく損傷したため修復できなかった。新しい風見鶏の内部には、大火災をまぬかれた遺物や、大聖堂の再建に携わった約2,000人の名前が記された封書が収められている。

AFP/AFLO

A Fashion Icon

Jane Birkin brought joy to people around the world

■ ジェーン・バーキン
ジェーン・バーキンの葬儀はパリのサン＝ロック教会で行われた。葬儀にはフランス大統領夫人のブリジット・マクロンや、ファッションブランド「サンローラン」の関係者など多くの著名人が参列した。

gettyimages

In the 1960s and 1970s, there was a global boom in French music and films. One of the biggest stars from that era was Jane Birkin. She was born in London in 1946 and grew up in the wealthy Chelsea area. As a young girl, she was very thin. Her classmates bullied her and called her "half boy, half girl." She was discouraged, but she followed her dreams. At the age of 20, she started acting in films. She and French director Serge Gainsbourg married and made many songs that became hits throughout the world. After she became a star, she worked mostly in France.

NOTES

00. icon [áikɑn]
   熱愛や崇拝の対象となる人
11. director [dəréktər] （映画）監督
20. Jean-Louis Dumas
   ジャン・ルイ・デュマ
20. the Executive Chairman　会長
21. Hermès
   エルメス（ファッションブランド名）
27. baby bottle　哺乳瓶
33. the Great East Japan Earthquake
   東日本大震災
36. evacuation center
   避難所、避難場所

■ ジェーン・バーキン（左）とセルジュ・ゲンスブール（1970年頃撮影）
2人は1968年制作の映画『スローガン』で出会った。1980年に破局するまで、世間の注目を集めた。

shutterstock/AFLO

Throughout the 1970s, Jane Birkin was an international fashion icon. In fact, the world's most famous bag takes its name from her. One day in the early 1980s, Birkin was on a plane to London. By chance, Jean-Louis Dumas, the Executive Chairman of Hermès, was also on that flight. Birkin had a young child at the time, and she told Dumas that she wished she had a fashionable yet convenient bag to carry her things. She gave Dumas an idea for a bag that was simple, attractive, and could hold baby bottles. Hermès started producing this bag in 1984, and it became a huge hit. Hermès paid her a fee each year to use her name, much of which was donated to charities chosen by Birkin.

Jane Birkin also became famous for her charity work. Right after the Great East Japan Earthquake in March 2011, she came to Japan to help people in the disaster areas. She visited evacuation centers and performed a concert in Shibuya. At that time, many people were reluctant to visit Japan due to the Fukushima nuclear accident, and overseas artists cancelled their trips. Although she was suffering from cancer at the time, she was one of the first overseas artists to come to Japan after the earthquake.

Her support for charities and human rights continued until her death in July 2023. Before she passed away, she was asked why she worked so hard throughout her lifetime. "That's because I can't stop," she said. "As long as I can help a little, even a little tiny bit... I will continue my work." ■

■ 渋谷パルコPART1 前での募金活動の様子（2011年4月6日）
アカペラで1曲歌った後、募金箱を手にしたジェーンは、自らお札を2枚募金箱に入れて来場者に募金を呼びかけた。ジェーンはこの日の前日に来日したばかりだった。

shutterstock/AFLO

WANT TO LEARN MORE?

Website　エルメス　バーキン - https://www.hermes.com/jp/ja/content/297706-birkin/
Book　山口 路子著『ジェーン・バーキンの言葉』大和書房
Book　ジャンヌ・ダマス他著『パリと生きる女たち』アノニマ・スタジオ

VOICE DL

Powering the Future

Our society needs electricity. But how should we make it?

■ Google 社のデータセンター（アメリカ、ジョージア州）
データセンター内に配置されているコンピューターサーバーの性能は以前と比べ飛躍的に向上し、演算装置である CPU や GPU の消費電力量も年々増大している。消費電力量の増大に比例してサーバーの発熱量も増えるため、データセンター内の温度と湿度を一定に保つための空調や冷却水に必要な電力も増大し続けている。

Camera Press/AFLO

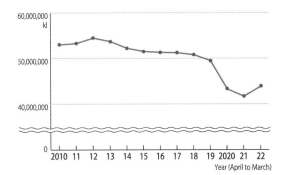

■ Graph 1 : Total fuel consumed by cars in Japan
2020年度、2021年度の燃料消費量の大きな落ち込みは、新型コロナウイルス感染症の影響によると考えられている。

Electricity is essential for modern society. It is used for transportation, heating, lighting, communication, computing, and other essential services. As these services are used in a growing range of applications, their importance continues to grow. While oil and coal exist in nature, electricity does not. It is a physical phenomenon, so it must be produced to be used. Supplying electricity stably and at low cost is one of society's greatest challenges.

Until around 2010, Japan was relatively optimistic about its stable supply of electricity. This was because people thought that demand for electricity, like other forms of energy, would fall significantly. This was based on two factors: a decrease in population and improved energy efficiency through technological innovation. In fact, as shown in Graph 1, the total fuel consumption of cars in Japan decreased from 2012 to 2019, the year before the COVID-19 pandemic began. This is despite the fact that the total number of cars in Japan increased during the same period. Fuel consumption decreased because of the increase in hybrid cars and improved fuel efficiency due to advances in engine technology. Similarly, the consumption of electricity is decreasing due to developments in voltage control technology, which is used in devices from railroad cars to electrical appliances. Today's railroad cars, refrigerators, and air conditioners require around 30 to 50% less electricity than models made until around 2000. In total, Japan's electricity demand has been decreasing slightly in recent years.

■ 新幹線 N700S 系（左）と 0 系（右）
0系新幹線は1964年から2008年まで運用された。0系の最高速度は220km/hだったが、2020年から運用されている最新型車両のN700S系は360km/hである。また、N700S系は0系の約51%の消費電力量で運行している。

NOTES

02. heating [híːtiŋ] 暖房
03. computing [kəmpjúːtiŋ]（コンピューターの）演算
07. coal [kóul] 石炭
08. phenomenon [finámənàn] 現象
13. optimistic [àptəmístik] 楽観的な
16. significantly [signífikəntli] 著しく
30. voltage [vóultidʒ] 電圧
32. railroad [réilròud] 鉄道（の）
32. electrical appliance 電化製品

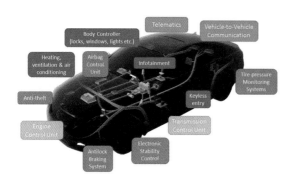

■ 車載 ECU (Electronic Control Unit) の種類

衝突軽減ブレーキ等の安全機能や自動運転機能、盗難防止機能などの先進機能が搭載されている車は、搭載された ECU と呼ばれる電子制御コンピューターで制御されている。

However, a growing number of experts believe that Japan's electricity demand is likely to increase. One reason is that reducing CO_2 has become a global goal, so electricity is being used as an alternative to fossil fuels. For example, there has been a shift from gasoline vehicles that emit CO_2 to EVs that run on electric motors. The percentage of EVs in Japan's total vehicle population is likely to grow, as it has in China and Europe. In addition, electricity is increasingly being used for boilers that produce hot water and steam for factories and other facilities.

The second reason that Japan's electricity demand may increase is the development of IT. Nowadays, not only mobile phones and computers but also electrical appliances are connected to networks, and new technologies such as AI are being used. New cars also depend on networks. Compared to cars produced before 2010, many cars today use more advanced software to improve fuel efficiency, safety, and comfort. Data from the car is collected by the automaker's data center over a network and analyzed by AI, and the car is updated with new software. Naturally, the more things that are connected to the network, the more data flows through the network, and the more data centers there will be to process the collected data. Data centers accounted for 1% of the world's electricity consumption in 2017, but just five years later, this number had risen to 4%. And if information technology advances further, electricity consumption is likely to increase even more rapidly.

As demand for electricity increases, supplying electricity at low cost becomes

NOTES

42. alternative [ɔːltə́ːrnətiv] 代替物
43. fossil fuel 化石燃料
44. emit [imít] 放出する
45. EV 電気自動車
45. motor [móutər] モーター
49. boiler [bɔ́ilər] ボイラー
50. steam [stíːm] 蒸気

58. AI 人工知能
63. automaker [ɔ́ːtoumèikər] 自動車メーカー
65. update [ʌ̀pdéit] 更新する
79. solar power 太陽光発電
79. wind power 風力発電
80. promising [práməsiŋ] 前途有望

な、期待できる
91. power plant 発電所
96. power outage 停電
102. thermal power 地熱発電
104. nuclear power 原子力発電
112. revolutionary [rèvəl(j)úːʃənèri] 革命的な、画期的な

■ メガソーラー
全国でメガソーラーが急速に増えている要因の1つは、一般建築物の建設時に必要な耐震性等の基準が、メガソーラー建設時には適用されないことである。そのため、土砂崩れや火災による被害が全国各地で深刻化している。

more difficult. Solar and wind power are promising, but it is not likely that they could cover all of our needs. Of course, generating electricity using solar and wind power, which nature provides for free, is a good option. However, these methods make it difficult to supply the required amount of electricity at the time it is needed. The cost of storing electricity is very high, so electricity must be generated at the same time it is used. In other words, the electricity we need to use now must be generated at a power plant right now. For this reason, power companies are checking electricity demand 24 hours a day and carefully controlling the amount of electricity they generate. This is because power outages occur not only when the amount of electricity generated is too low to meet demand, but also when the amount of electricity generated is too high.

Each of the main power generation methods currently in use has advantages and disadvantages. Thermal power generation makes it easy to control the amount of power generated but produces CO_2. Nuclear power generation is low-cost and can generate large amounts of power, but in the event of a major accident, the damage could be greater than with other methods. Solar and wind power can generate electricity without using fossil fuels, but they make it difficult to supply power steadily. Ideally, revolutionary technology would overcome these disadvantages or make it possible to store huge amounts of electricity at low costs. But for now, we will need a combination of different power generation methods to supply electricity. ■

■ 福島第一原子力発電所の事故（2011年3月15日撮影）
東日本大震災により発生したこの事故は、国際原子力事象評価尺度において最高レベルの7に分類されている。現在、レベル7に分類されている事故は1986年のチェルノブイリ（チョルノービリ）原子力発電所事故と福島の事故の2つのみとなっている。

WANT TO LEARN MORE?

Website	経済産業省　資源エネルギー庁 - https://www.enecho.meti.go.jp/
Book	木舟 辰平著『電力システムの基本と仕組みがよ〜くわかる本』秀和システム
Book	宇佐美 典也著『電力危機 私たちはいつまで高い電気代を払い続けるのか？』星海社

VOICE D1

The Next Step in Design

■ 2020 東京五輪開会式で披露されたサーフィンのピクトグラムの演出
ユニバーサルデザインの１つであるピクトグラムは、1964 年開催の東京五
輪で誕生し、競技を含む 39 種類が作られた。当時は外国人観光客が現在ほ
ど多くなく、多言語の案内板がほとんどなかった。

新華社 /AFLO

Media Universal Design can help everyone get important information

When we look around us, we take in a lot of information. But does everyone really understand it all? Can the elderly, children, people with disabilities, and people from other countries receive the information in the same way? To help make sure that important information is clear to everyone, there is a new approach called "media universal design (MUD)." It comes from a concept called Color Universal Design, which was created for people who have trouble distinguishing the differences between colors. That concept was expanded to include text and other elements of design. MUD improves

NOTES

04. disability [dìsəbíləti] 障がい
09. concept [kánsept] 概念、考え
14. element [éləmənt] 要素
21. background [bǽkgràund] 背景
22. color vision problem 色覚の問題
29. letter [létər] 文字

29. line [láin] 行
30. UD font UD フォント (書体)
42. emergency [imə́ːrdʒənsi]
    緊急 (事態)
43. hazard map ハザードマップ
45. emergency exit 非常口

45. certain [sə́ːrtn]
    ある程度の、一定の
47. a matter of life and death
    生死に関わる重大問題

the designs we see in everyday life so that information is easy for everyone to understand.

There are three key points to MUD. The first is to make colors easier to see. For example, reading green text on a red background can be very difficult for some people. This kind of color vision problem affects about one in 20 men and one in 500 women in Japan, and it is even more common in other countries. MUD uses other colors, patterns, and designs to make colors clearer. The second point is to make text easier to read. One way is to make text larger and put more space between letters and lines. Another way is to use UD fonts. These fonts are often used for educational and public documents because the characters are easy to

Normal color vision　　　**Color vision problem**

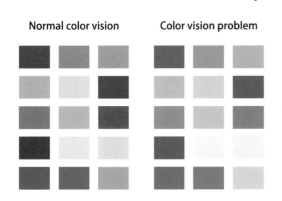

■ 一般の人と色覚に障がいを持つ人の見え方の違い
色覚に障がいを持つ人の見え方は個人差があるが、一般的には「青と紫」「深緑と茶色」「淡い水色と淡いピンク」の組み合わせや、彩度の低い色の組み合わせが識別しにくいと言われている。

Normal color vision　　　**Color vision problem**

■ MUD を取り入れて作成されたグラフ（左）と、色覚障がいを持つ人の同グラフの見え方（右）
先天性色覚障がいは、性染色体（男性 XY、女性 XX）の X 染色体の遺伝子が原因の 1 つである。男性の場合は X 染色体に色覚障がいの遺伝子があれば発症する。女性の場合は両方の X 染色体に色覚障がいの遺伝子があれば発症すると言われている。

read. The third is to make symbols and other displays easier to understand. Some words may be too difficult for children or for people who speak a different language. By using simple pictures and words, everyone can get the same information.

The MUD approach to design is necessary for information such as street signs, product guides, and textbooks. It is especially important for emergency information. This includes hazard maps, which use colors to show the impact of natural disasters. Emergency exits also use certain colors and symbols. In emergencies, information can be a matter of life and death. Everyone sees the world differently, so we need to reduce these differences. ■

WANT TO LEARN MORE?

Website	NPO 法人メディア・ユニバーサル・デザイン協会 - https://www.media-ud.org/
Book	教育出版 CUD 事務局著『カラーユニバーサルデザインの手引き』教育出版
Book	市川一夫著『知られざる色覚異常の真実』幻冬舎

VOICE DL

Northern Lights

A new project in Europe aims to reduce CO₂ in the air

■ **北海道・苫小牧の CCS 実証実験施設**

日本初の CCS 大規模実証実験は国家プロジェクトとして実施された。2016 年度より 1 日約 600 トンの CO₂ の地下への圧入が開始され、2019 年 11 月 22 日には、目標とした累計 30 万トンの CO₂ の圧入が完了した。現在は圧入を停止してモニタリングが行われている。

毎日新聞社 /AFLO

Climate change is a challenge that affects every country and every person in the world. The Paris Agreement adopted in 2015 gives targets for reducing the increase in global average temperatures. To achieve these targets, countries will have to reduce their CO₂ emissions. One of the ways to do this is a technology called Carbon dioxide Capture

05

NOTES

03. agreement [əgríːmənt] 協定
04. target [tɑ́rgit] 目標
07. emission [imíʃən] 排出
08. carbon dioxide 二酸化炭素

08. capture [kǽptʃər] (名) 捕獲、取り込み　(動) 取り込む
12. layer [léiər] 層、地層
26. Norwegian [nɔːrwíːdʒən] ノルウェーの

27. fertilizer [fɔ́ːrtəlàizər] 肥料
36. ocean floor 海底
50. fossil fuel 化石燃料
51. renewable energy 再生可能エネルギー

and Storage (CCS).

With CCS, CO_2 is collected by separating it from other gases and changing it into liquid. The liquid CO_2 is stored in holes in layers of rock at least one kilometer underground. This CO_2 is trapped by the layers above it. Studies have shown that CO_2 can be safely stored underground for thousands of years if it is managed properly. However, the technology requires lots of money and knowledge, so there are only a few such projects now in the world.

One major CCS project in Europe is called Northern Lights. This is a partnership between several energy companies, and some money is given by the government of Norway. In 2022, Northern Lights signed an agreement with a Norwegian company called Yara. Yara makes fertilizer and has factories in many countries. Fertilizer is important for farming, but producing and using it creates a lot of CO_2. Under this agreement, Northern Lights will capture about 800,000 tons of CO_2 each year from Yara's plant in the Netherlands. It will then send the liquid CO_2 to a site in the Norwegian North Sea, where it will be put 2,600 meters below the ocean floor. This is the world's first CO_2

■CO₂注入後（上）と注入前（下）の岩石のサンプル
CO₂を注入する岩石は砂岩や玄武岩などの隙間の多い種類が適している。玄武岩は世界の海底の大部分と、大陸の岩石の約10％を占めている。アイスランドで行われた実験では、玄武岩に注入されたCO₂の95％が2年以内に固形化したことが報告されている。　　AP/AFLO

transport agreement between countries. The project hopes to capture 1.5 million tons of CO_2 when it begins operations in 2024 and more in the following years.

Although CCS is thought to be safe, there are many concerns about it. One is that the CO_2 could gradually come out of the underground rocks. This could pollute water supplies or add more CO_2 to the air. Another is that pressure is created when CO_2 is placed deep underground. This pressure could eventually cause earthquakes. In addition, if CCS becomes available, companies may be more likely to continue using fossil fuels rather than switching to renewable energy. As one possible solution for climate change, CCS will have to be studied and performed very carefully. ■

WANT TO LEARN MORE?
Website Northern Lights（英語）- https://norlights.com/
Website 経済産業省　資源エネルギー庁 - https://www.enecho.meti.go.jp/
Book 柳 憲一郎他編『脱炭素とCCS － 二酸化炭素回収貯留の法政策』信山社

VOICE DL

The Power of Thinking

Can generative AI replace humans?

■ 生成 AI「Midjourney」により作成された画像

AI（人工知能）という言葉は 1956 年に開催されたダートマス会議で初めて、人間のように考える機械のことを指す言葉として使用された。現在、生成 AI は「ChatGPT」に代表される対話型 AI や、Google が運営する音楽生成型 AI の「Music LM」、プログラミング言語生成や画像・動画生成 AI など多くの種類がある。

■ Open AI 社の動画生成 AI「Sora」

2024 年 2 月に発表された「Sora」は、「渋谷の交差点で多くの人が道路を横断している動画を作って」などとテキストを入力するだけで、最長 1 分の動画を作ることができるツール。

CFoto/AFLO

Artificial intelligence (AI) is a technology that allows computers to perform the intellectual activities of humans. These are activities that use the human brain, such as writing sentences and talking to people. AI studies large amounts of data related to such activities and finds rules from it. Then, based on those rules, it selects the appropriate answer to a given problem. It can also generate new data and rules based on the data and patterns it learns.

Generative AI is a type of artificial intelligence. It can create new content in response to human requests based on the data it has learned. It can create not only text, but also music, images, and even videos. For example, if a person types "I want to know more about the American college entrance examination system" into a generative AI program, it will respond with text or audio. Furthermore, if you ask, "I want you to create music to match this beautiful landscape video," the generative AI will generate music content.

Generative AI has greatly changed the way we think about computers. Before AI, many people thought that it was impossible for computers to do creative work by themselves. To most people, computers were simply machines that

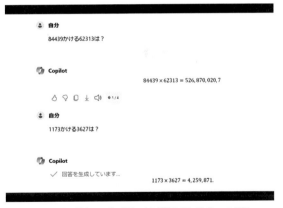

■ Microsoft 社の検索エンジン「Bing」に搭載された AI チャット機能「Copilot」の計算間違い

生成 AI は簡単に使えて、さまざまな要求に応える便利なツールだが、現状では 4 桁× 4 桁の掛け算をさせてみるとほぼ間違えてしまう。また、学習時のデータのボリュームが少なかったり、誤情報が含まれていると、虚偽の情報を生成してしまうことがある。

NOTES

- 00. generative AI　生成 AI
- 01. artificial intelligence (AI)　人工知能
- 03. intellectual [ìntəléktʃuəl] 知的な
- 06. large amounts of ～　大量の～
- 10. generate [dʒénərèit] 生成する
- 14. content [kántent] コンテンツ（電子的に利用可能な画像、動画、情報）、（本や雑誌の）内容
- 14. in response to ～　～に応えて
- 24. match [mǽtʃ] 調和する
- 24. landscape [lǽndskèip]　風景、景色
- 31. simply [símpli] 単に、～だけ

could do tasks much faster than humans. For example, they could quickly search for pages that contain a certain word from a huge number of websites, or they could perform complex calculations. However, generative AI can now create things in ways similar to humans.

In recent years, generative AI has been widely used by creative fields. One example is the world of advertising. Generative AI can quickly create a large amount of advertising text, such as product slogans and explanations, at almost no cost. Therefore, some companies have decided that it is more efficient to create many samples with generative AI and select the best ones from those. Because of this, some copywriters have lost their jobs. The writing created by generative AI is often of lower quality than the work of experienced copywriters. However, cost and speed are important factors for business.

Generative AI is also being used in scientific research. Typically, scientists need to review past academic papers and experimental data from many years. Then they use this knowledge to develop new research models. By conducting experiments and research, they add to existing knowledge. However, generative AI can analyze large amounts of academic papers and experimental data much faster than humans. And it can quickly create large numbers of new research models based on this learning.

There are several problems with generative AI. The biggest problem is that the content of what is generated may contain incorrect information. This is because there may be incorrect information in the data that generative AI learns from. It is not yet able to judge whether

■ 自民党本部での勉強会に参加した堀江貴文氏（左）と前澤友作氏（右）
SNSで著名人の画像や名前を無断使用し、投資などを呼びかける『なりすまし広告』を使った詐欺事件が発生している。ZOZO創業者で起業家の前澤友作氏、実業家の堀江貴文氏らが被害に遭っている。広告に使われている画像や音声は、生成AIで作成されたものもある。
毎日新聞社/AFLO

NOTES
34. certain [sə́ːrtn] 特定の、とある
36. complex [kὰmpléks] 複雑な
36. calculation [kæ̀lkjəléiʃən] 計算、演算
41. advertising [ǽdvərtàiziŋ] 広告 (の)
43. product slogan キャッチコピー
49. copywriter [kápiràitər] コピーライター（宣伝文句を作成する人）
52. experienced [ikspíəriənst] 経験豊富な
56. scientific [sàiəntífik] 科学の
57. academic paper 学術論文
58. experimental [ikspèrəméntl] 実験の
77. the University of Tokyo 東京大学
98. background [bǽkgràund] 背景

■ AI 戦略会議に参加した松尾豊教授

AI 戦略会議は、AI 規制に関する国際的な議論を円滑に進めることや、国内のルールづくりを主導する役割を担う目的で 2023 年 5 月に政府により立ち上げられた。

毎日新聞社 /AFLO

75 the information it learns is correct or not. Furthermore, according to Professor Yutaka Matsuo of the University of Tokyo, generative AI programs tend to give results that are pleasing to the people who use 80 them. This is because generative AI also learns how people responded to things that were created in the past. In other words, generative AI thinks that things that got positive responses from people are correct. 85 For example, if you ask a generative AI program for its opinion about a report you wrote, it will likely give a few gentle opinions. However, if you tell the generative AI program that the same report 90 was written by one of your rivals, it often points out many more problems.

Will generative AI take away our jobs? It is true that some advertising copywriters and science laboratory assistants may be replaced by AI. News writers who create 95 articles based on government reports are also likely to lose their jobs. In addition, some of the background music for videos online will probably be created by generative AI instead of human musicians. 100 However, today's generative AI is just a tool that can produce what people want quickly, in large quantities, and at low cost. It is still difficult for generative AI to judge whether what it produces is correct 105 or of good quality. For that reason, in all fields, including advertising and scientific research, humans will need to review what generative AI creates. In other words, there will still be jobs for true experts and 110 creators. ■

Reason	
Market / Economic Conditions	221,691
No Reason	75,723
Closing	75,053
Cost-Cutting	58,248
Restructuring	36,729
Artificial Intelligence	**3,967**
Outsourcing Operations Outside the US	2,000
COVID-19	414

■ 失業の理由

アメリカの再就職支援会社チャレンジャー・グレイ＆クリスマスの報告書によれば、2023 年 1 月から 8 月末まで 8 か月間で、AI の台頭により失業した人は約 4,000 人と発表された。

出典：2023　Challenger, Gray & Christmas,Inc

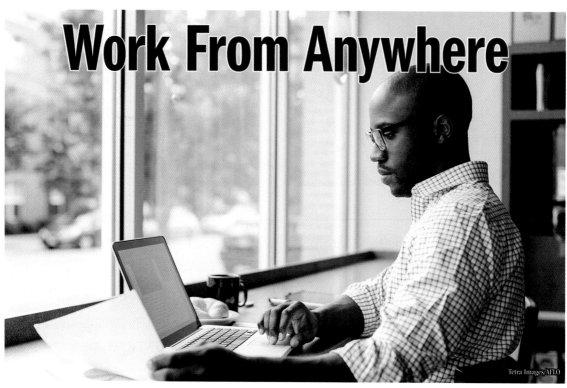

Work From Anywhere

Tetra Images/AFLO

Japan may give visas to "digital nomads"

During the COVID-19 pandemic, "work-from-home" became a popular trend. For workers whose jobs can be done online, the new trend is "work-from-anywhere." This means that people can do their work remotely from any location in the world, not just home. All they need is a computer, an internet connection, and their skills. These workers are called "digital nomads."

There are about 35 million digital nomads in the world, and that number could reach 1 billion in the 2030s.

The digital nomad style of working has benefits for both workers and companies. Workers can try living in a comfortable resort area or an exciting city. They can also move from place to place easily. About 66% of digital nomads stay in one location

NOTES

00. digital nomado デジタルノマド （nomad は「遊牧民」の意味）	リモートで、ネット経由で
01. COVID-19 pandemic 新型コロナウイルスの感染拡大	30. local economy 地域経済
	31. housing [háuziŋ] 住宅、住居
06. remotely [rimóutli]	34. gap [gǽp] 格差、溝
	36. rent [rént] 家賃

41. skilled [skíld] 技術を持った、熟練の
49. working visa 就労ビザ
50. Japan-based 日本を拠点とする
55. Germany [dʒə́ːrməni] ドイツ

Digital Nomad Countries of Origin

- The U.S. 31%
- Other 35 countries 49%
- Portugal 8%
- Germany 7%
- Brazil 5%

Average yearly income

- ~ $24,999 — 6%
- $25,000 ~ $49,999 — 18%
- $50,000 ~ $99,999 — 34%
- $100,000 ~ $249,999 — 34%
- $250,000 ~ — 8%

Top job types

1st	Marketing
2nd	IT/Software Development
3rd	Digital Design
4th	Writing (author, copywriter)
5th	E-Commerce*
6th	Information Technology
7th	Photography
8th	Online Assistant

*Buying and selling things using the internet

■ デジタルノマドに関するデータ

出典：A Brother Abroad　63 Surprising Digital Nomad Statistics in 2022

for around three to six months. They can also live in their hometowns if they need to care for family members. Companies benefit because they have more workers to choose from. If the work can be done remotely, the company does not have to hire a person near their office.

There are positive and negative effects for the areas where many digital nomads stay. Many digital nomads live in parts of Asia or Latin America where the cost of living is low. They help local economies by paying for food and housing. However, digital nomads usually earn higher salaries than the locals in such areas. This can worsen the gap between rich and poor people. For example, apartment owners may raise their rents if many digital nomads come to their area. If this happens, it will be more difficult for local people to afford housing with their salaries.

The Japanese government sees benefits from the digital nomad trend. Skilled workers from other countries could help the economy. To bring more digital nomads, Japan changed its visa system. Before this change, people from most countries could stay in Japan for only 90 days without a visa. If a person wanted to stay for longer than 90 days, they had to get a working visa. However, they could only get this visa if they work for a Japan-based company. This made it difficult for many digital nomads to get visas. The new system allows digital nomads to stay in Japan for six months without working visas. Today, more than 50 countries including Germany and Australia offer digital nomad visas. Japan's new visa system may bring more digital nomads to Japan. ■

Landing on the Moon

■ SLIM の月面着陸イメージ

SLIM は 2024 年 1 月 24 日午前 0 時より、約 20 分かけて月面着陸を実施した。月面への降下中にメインエンジン 2 基のうち 1 基が故障し、噴射口が脱落した。その影響で着陸イメージとは異なり、実際には逆立ちするような姿勢で着陸した。

JAXA

The SLIM project is an important first for Japan's space program

Humans on Earth have turned more attention toward space in recent years. Satellites have become more and more important for communications. There may be resources in space that we can use on Earth. And some people even believe we may need to live on other planets if we cannot live on Earth. With all of this in mind, a new race has started to put spacecraft on the Moon.

JAXA developed a project called SLIM (Smart Lander for Investigating Moon). The lander was launched in September 2023 and landed on the Moon on January 20, 2024. With this landing, Japan became

NOTES

03. satellite [sǽtəlàit] 衛星
04. communications [kəmjùːnəkéiʃənz] 通信（手段）
08. with ~ in mind ～を念頭に置いて
09. spacecraft [spéiskrὰft] 宇宙探査機

11. Smart Lander for Investigating Moon 小型月着陸実証機
15. soft lunar touchdown 月面軟着陸
18. pinpoint lunar landing ピンポイント月面着陸
21. target [tάːrgit] 目標

23. crater [kréitər] クレーター
31. solar-powered battery 太陽電池
32. at an angle 傾斜して
52. desirably [dizáiərəbli] 願わくは、望ましくは
53. unexplored [Àniksplɔ́ːrd] 未踏の

the fifth country to make a successful "soft lunar touchdown." The first four were the Soviet Union, the United States, China, and India. SLIM was designed for pinpoint lunar landing. In the past, spacecraft landed on the Moon where it was easy to land, which was usually several kilometers from the target. The goal with SLIM was to land within 100 meters of the target. The target was a crater with rocks to be studied. These rocks are believed to be from inside the Moon. SLIM was able to land just 55 meters from its target. After it landed, it successfully took photographs of the rocks.

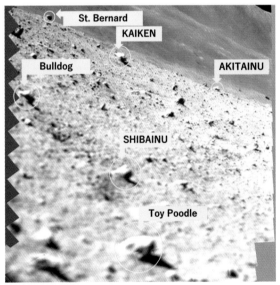

■ SLIM により撮影された月面の岩石
観測対象の岩石には、それぞれの相対的な大きさが把握しやすいよう犬種の名前がつけられた。月の誕生については諸説あり、その1つに原始の地球に惑星が衝突して分裂し月ができたとする「ジャイアントインパクト説」がある。月の岩石の成分が地球内部の層の成分と似ていれば、ジャイアントインパクト説を補強できる可能性がある。
JAXA/ 立命館大学 / 会津大学

Despite SLIM's successful landing, scientists were worried about some things. The first problem was SLIM's solar-powered battery. SLIM landed at an angle, and its solar panels were facing west. Because it could not get sunlight at first, JAXA switched its power off a few hours after landing. They wondered if it would turn on again. However, when the Sun's angle changed, SLIM began its observations. After about three days of work, it went to sleep. Then came the second problem, which was the long and cold lunar nights. On the Moon, there are about 15 days of daytime and then about 15 days of nighttime. During the nighttime, the temperature drops to below minus 130 degrees. SLIM was not designed to survive such cold temperatures. However, to JAXA's surprise, SLIM started working again after its long sleep.

JAXA says that the work SLIM has already performed is a huge success. "This will inspire more and more people, desirably Japanese missions, to try to land on unexplored places on the Moon," said the project manager. More private companies will be working to develop space vehicles in the future. ■

WANT TO LEARN MORE?
Website JAXA（国立研究開発法人宇宙航空研究開発機構） https://www.jaxa.jp/
Book トーマス・J・ケリー著『月着陸船開発物語』プレアデス出版
Book 寺薗 淳也著『夜ふかしするほど面白い「月の話」』PHP 研究所

VOICE DL

本書の「解答解説書（付録）」および「課題テスト（付録）」は、先生からのお申し出をいただいたときに限り、お届け致します。

■ 写真・資料図版提供（順不同、敬称略）
AFLO ほか

■ CD ナレーション
Kevin Glenz ほか

■ 表紙写真
アメリカ合衆国議会議事堂
Adobe Stock

NEWSBREAKS
for STANDARD English Learners
2024

ニュースブレイク 2024 年 **スタンダード**
定価 600 円＋税
付録【設問集・解答解説書・課題テスト】

初刷発行：2024 年 6 月 3 日
2 刷発行：2024 年 6 月 24 日

本 書 著 者　Kevin Glenz・小林義昌

編 集 協 力　田澤仁
発 行 所　株式会社 エミル出版

本社　〒 102-0072　東京都千代田区飯田橋 2-8-1
　　　【電　　　話】03-6272-5481
　　　【ファックス】03-6272-5482